A National Trust Series

Long Distance Flyers

THE INSIDE STORY OF
BIRD MIGRATION

Harry T Sutton

BATSFORD – HERITAGE BOOKS

Research: R J Sutton

Design and art direction: Fetherstonhaugh Associates, London

Illustrations: Chapter 1, Petula Stone; Chapters 2 and 3, Valerie Headland, Judith Jeffery, Jane Morgan and Petula Stone

Copyright © 1978 by B T Batsford Limited and Heritage Books

Produced by Heritage Books

Published jointly by B T Batsford Limited and Heritage Books

Distributed by B T Batsford Limited, 4 Fitzhardinge Street, London W1H 0AH

Printed by Robert MacLehose & Co. Ltd, Glasgow

ISBN 0 7134 1728 5

Contents

The publishers wish to thank David Musson of the National Trust for the
valuable advice he gave in the writing of this book.

1 Last One Flies South

It had been a fine, warm summer with plenty of insects for birds to eat. In a barn near a quiet-flowing stream, a pair of Swallows had raised three separate broods and there had been plenty of food for them all. The nest, cleverly made with mud from the river bank and lined with moss and feathers, was on a beam which spanned the high barn roof. When sitting on her eggs, the mother bird was snug and warm inside the barn even if it was cold and wet outside.

The parent birds were proud of their healthy brood and took great care that they would grow up fine strong Swallows like themselves. It was hard work, catching flies and feeding them to their ever-hungry young. But it did not take long for the fledglings to grow their feathers and leave the nest. In no time they were all able to swoop and dart along the river bank catching flies for themselves. All, that is, except one. That was Last One – who simply would not leave the nest.

It could have been that Last One was lazy. Or perhaps he was just not as bright as the rest. Whatever the reason, and even though the parent birds called and called to urge him out, he would not budge an inch. He simply stayed inside, crying out for food until one of the Swallows gave in and took him a beakful of insects to keep him quiet.

It would not have mattered but for one important fact. Each year, towards the end of August, the evenings in Britain grow shorter and there is a chilly feeling in the air. This is a warning to the birds that winter is not far off with icy winds and frost and snow. There will be no insects then for birds to eat. Nor juicy fruits or tasty seeds. For some birds, of course – House Sparrows, Owls and Woodpeckers for example – this does not matter for they are able to find enough food at any time of the year. But for the Swallows who live only on insects such as gnats and flies and beetles, it was a very serious matter indeed. Directly they felt the cold and saw the sunsets coming earlier every day, they became nervous and jumpy. They began to eat more than usual and a little voice inside them seemed to say: 'Fly away – fly away! The cold is coming. Fly away!'

The Swallows were not the only birds to be worried and upset. Cuckoos, Swifts, Yellow Wagtails and a dozen other kinds of bird were eating all the food they could find and they were all beginning to hear that little bird voice saying: 'Fly away. The cold is coming. Fly away!'

Inside the barn, Last One must have heard that little voice for one morning, without even being called by the parent birds, he flew out of the nest and with one long swoop and a quick climb outside, he was on top of the barn roof. Perching rather shakily at first, his new feathers ruffled, he scolded and grumbled until his patient mother came to him with a delicious bundle of insects in her beak. So perhaps Last One would be in time for the great Fly Away after all!

After only a few days, Last One could fly and catch insects as cleverly as his brothers and sisters who had left the nest before him. His parents still brought him food for a time, hovering in flight to give him those juicy beaksful of flies that he liked so much. But soon he was able to look after himself and how he enjoyed those flashing darts, just above the smooth waters of the stream, scooping flies and gnats into his wide open mouth!

One day, when he was out hunting for flies, Last One had an adventure. He had strayed away from the rest of the birds when, looking down, he saw a new part of the river where he had never been before. There seemed to be plenty of insects, flying beetles and river flies buzzing amongst the reeds along the banks. So down he swooped. Then he levelled off to fly low along the bank – and the next thing he knew, he was caught in a net! It had such a fine mesh that he simply had not seen it there. And now he was caught. Just when all the other Swallows were ready for the great Fly Away!

Last One could not know, of course, but the man who

gently took him from the net was an ornithologist – one who studies birds – and when, a few minutes later, he was released to fly back to the barn, he had a little metal ring round one of his legs. It was a pity that Last One did not understand for he was now number HS 89702 and if ever he was caught again that number would be written down and a letter would be sent to the ornithologist telling him where he had been caught. He was now a Very Important Bird. But he knew nothing about all that. Nor did he care. He was just happy to be out of the net and free once more to fly, carefree and happy, along the river near the barn.

It was now early September and Swallows from all along the river were gathering together, roosting in great numbers in the reeds and perching in rows along telephone wires, fence tops and in the trees. They were all well fed at the end of their summer stay but now the time had finally come for the long Fly Away – away from the cold that would soon grip all the northern lands.

The fly away – migration – began one fine morning just after dawn when the sky was clear and there was just a slight breeze from the north east. Almost as though somebody had fired a starting pistol for a race, most of the Swallows along the river for several miles took off in a great swirling cloud, made a circling flight over the lush river valley where they had spent their warm summer months, and then, just as though one of them had given the order, they all turned and flew south.

Last One, of course, was one of them, his little metal ring tucked up on his leg as he flew with the rest of the Swallow flock over the green English countryside. The barn by the river where Last One's adventure began, was in Norfolk, just outside the city of Norwich, a pleasant place of small farms, country churches and village schools. The place they were going to was not in the least like that. There was certainly a river with reed beds and plenty of insects buzzing above the water, but there were no church spires or barns or farms, or

even fields. They were flying to South Africa, more than five thousand miles away and in between there were seas and deserts to cross, headwinds and storms to meet and many other dangers on the way. Last One did not know that, of course, or else he might have been tempted to turn round and spend the winter in that warm barn where he was born! Instead, he just flew on amongst the thousands of other Swallows travelling along, just above tree-top height, on their way towards the sun which was already high above the horizon to the south.

Even though there was such a long journey ahead of them, the Swallows did not hurry. They flew steadily over the sunlit fields, stopping now and then, a great swirl of wings out of the sky, to take a quick mouthful of flies – and then off again southwards, always towards the south. By nightfall they had travelled only a hundred miles when the time came for them to roost. Swallows fly mostly by day in their long flights to Africa although they can also fly at night if there is a need. Towards dusk, therefore, the leaders of the flock began to look for a suitable place to roost for the night and the best places were those already taken by Swallows that had not yet set off for the great Fly Away. Somewhere north of London, that fine summer night, some local Swallows peacefully roosting in the reeds and willows of a country stream were suddenly disturbed by the arrival of a few thousand visitors – come to stay for the night. And they had to make room for them – or be pushed off their own perches into the water below! Within minutes they had all settled in, the reeds were black with Swallows and the darkness became quiet with only an occasional splash of a water rat or the hoot of an owl to disturb the sleeping birds. Last One, asleep on a crowded willow stem, was tired after his first day of the great Fly Away south.

The next day, soon after dawn, the Swallows were away again on their leisurely flight, stopping now and then for a quick meal until they reached the south coast. Last One had never seen the sea and he would have liked to fly high above it – just in case he fell in. For even a young bird like him knew one thing perfectly well. Swallows can fly very well indeed – but not even the cleverest Swallow has ever learned to swim! To his surprise, however, all the older birds, instead of climbing, flew straight down close to the water until their wings almost touched the tops of the waves. He at once saw why this was, however, and he was soon skimming along the wave tops as easily as all the rest. The fact was that the wind had been behind them all the way down England but at the coast the wind was blowing inland from the sea. A headwind would slow them down and make the crossing longer; low down, the force of the wind was broken by the waves so that the Swallows could fly along, sheltered from its effects.

Last One was to learn many new things as he flew south. He discovered, for instance, that all the time the Swallows could see the sun they had no difficulty in finding the direction in which to fly. But if there was a fog or if the sky was overcast with thick cloud, they did not fly at all but stayed in one place, feeding and waiting for the fog or cloud to clear.

He also learned why the birds ate so much before they set off for the great Fly Away. Food means energy for a bird just as it does for us. To get fat is a way of storing up energy to use when there is a need and when food cannot be found. Camels, as everybody knows, store fat in their humps and can go for days without food or drink. Swallows travel mainly by day so that they can stop on the way to have a daily feed. They, therefore, do not need to get as fat as the birds who travel by day and by night. Some of these, for example the Nightingales, Turtle Doves and Cuckoos sometimes double their normal weight with fat when they get ready for their long flight. It is a wonder that some of them are able to fly at all!

But by far the most important thing that Last One learned was that, somehow, he was always quite sure about the direction in which he should fly. He had a feeling inside him which told him the way he should head even without the thousands of birds which were now flying together over the trees and fields of France. The position of the sun had something to do with it, he knew. He was also watching the ground with those bright, beady eyes so that he would recognise it if he flew over it another time. Last One, in fact, felt quite sure that even if he was left entirely by himself he would still be able to find his way to those distant reeds beside the river in South Africa. It was almost as though the memory of thousands of previous Fly Away journeys had been passed down to him by his parents and his parents' parents and his parents' parents' parents, right back through the centuries of Swallows which had made the same journey, long long ago.

It took the Swallows almost three weeks to make their unhurried way across France and Spain, stopping from time to time during the day to feed beside a river swamp or lake. Every night they crowded themselves in amongst the local

Swallows in some comfortable bed of reeds or willows. And every dawn they set off again flying south – always to the south.

When they reached the Mediterranean Sea, Last One was not in the least worried by the great sheet of water which stretched ahead, much further than his beady eyes could see. The other Swallows too, just flew straight on over the sea low down again, but this time for a different reason. Birds are not the only creatures to fly away from cold weather in the north. Butterflies and moths also fly to Africa for the winter months and the Swallows knew that they might find some on the way. Sure enough, halfway across they caught up with just such a cloud of butterflies and for a few minutes they delayed their flight to gobble up some of the delicious insects they loved so much to eat. As they swooped and turned, they were far too busy to notice that just below them there was a small islet – and living on the islet there was a colony of Falcons. And for a Falcon, a fat young Swallow makes a very tasty meal!

One of the Falcons had been hovering far above the Swallows, waiting for them to come within reach and now, seeing them busy eating butterflies, it made its deadly, killing swoop. Last One did not know this, of course, but he had flown a little apart from the other birds and he was now the target of that diving killer swooping down so menacingly from the empty sky. But another Swallow saw the danger and, screaming a quick warning, it dived towards the sea; the rest of the flock turned as one bird and followed. Last One had learned a lot since those lazy days in the nest and now, quick as a flash, he was diving too, just in time, for the Falcon's talons brushed his head as he reached the wave tops – and the Falcon had to end its dive to avoid hitting the sea. It had been a narrow escape – but there were many more dangers ahead for Last One before the journey's end.

When the Swallows reached the other side of the Mediterranean Sea, they were of course, in Africa. All the way through France and Spain they had been able to find food but now they had reached a land where the summer sun had burned the vegetation dry. There was no food to be had. Nor were there places to roost. So the Swallows simply flew on south, climbing higher and higher as they went.

Now, for the first time, Last One was to find out for himself just how valuable was that little reserve of fat he had built up during the flight over France and Spain. The Sahara Desert had now to be crossed, a vast expanse of sand and rock with no water, no trees, no grass. Only the blazing sun glaring down from an ever-cloudless sky from dawn to dusk. The birds would have to fly across it without stopping for a rest or for food. And the distance across was almost exactly equal to the distance they had already flown since they had left England, nearly 30 days before. They would have to fly that same distance now in only 30 hours!

It was early afternoon when the Swallows reached the desert. They flew high where there was a following wind to help them on their way. They were not alone for this was the meeting place for millions of birds from all over Europe, making their great Fly Away to the South. But those millions were spread wide across the whole Sahara. There was no easy route to follow from north to south.

Last One had become used to the southward flight. Each dawn the sun rose ahead of them and to the left as they flew. For a time then, the sun rose until it was directly in front of them and later it swung away to the right. Throughout the day the sun moved further and further to the right until, at dusk, it disappeared below the horizon almost directly behind. Last One had learned to know from the sun and the path it followed across the sky, exactly the direction he should fly. But now, as they reached the desert, the sun sank below the horizon and instead of looking for a place to roost, Last One found himself, with thousands of other birds, flying on into a darkening sky. It was the first time that he had ever flown at night!

At first Last One was confused by the fading light but when the sun had finally gone he looked up and there was the brightest of bright skies simply filled with sparkling stars! What is more, they too were moving, or seemed to move from left to right as had the sun. He saw at once that they had simply exchanged one sky pattern – the path of the sun – with another similar one – the paths of the stars. The direction in which to fly was as easily seen by night as by day. And so, over that great dry desert, the tiny Swallows from Norfolk flew steadily south. More than half a million wing movements would have to be made by each bird before they reached the other side. And there would be no food or drink to be had on the way!

The Swallows flew high in the cooler air above the desert. And they flew fast. The first, leisurely days of the Fly Away were over and Last One felt the sense of urgency which was now driving all the birds, their wings beating steadily, thousands of birds, beside him, in front and following behind. On, on, on, on – wings beating out the passing time. And never for one moment could they rest.

As he flew, Last One remembered those long, happy days at the barn. Planing along above the clear water of the stream, swerving perhaps to miss a Kingfisher darting by, a flash of blue, on its busy way down stream. The thought of the evenings when the bats came out and there was a friendly chase, round and round the barn, seeing who could make the steepest turn – the bats always won – until the young Swallows had to go to roost leaving the bats to hunt on all night alone. And he remembered the nest he was so loath to leave.

Those were the thoughts of Last One as he flew on and on, the stars bright above him and the sand, endless, empty, hostile, ever waiting down below.

When the sun rose at last, it was a great glare just to the left of their heading, for the Swallows were no longer flying south. They were crossing the desert towards the south east, a longer flight but one that was helped by a following wind and would end – for those that could last the course – in a countryside of stream and swamp. As they flew, the long day soon brought its losses. Some of the young birds had not built up enough reserves of fat. They were still growing and their food had been used for building bone and flesh with none over for fat. One by one they now began to fall behind, soon to drop and die on the sunbaked sand. Some older birds too, failed to reach the other side. Last One himself was wondering when the journey would ever end and doubting if his tired wings could carry him another mile – beating, beating, beating. And then, towards evening, there was a sudden quickening amongst the exhausted birds. They seemed to draw hidden energy and Last One felt himself gather speed as well. For there, still only a shadow in the desert ahead – there was a tree! Then another came in sight. Then a whole grove of trees and the glint of water. They were across.

The Swallows were still only halfway to South Africa, but the rest of the long flight was easy compared with the dangers of desert and sea. More Swallows were taken by birds of prey, Falcons, Harriers and Sparrowhawks, which hunted for food along the flight path of the migrant birds. Some others were lost in storms. For a few, the journey was just too long and they did not take off with the rest of the flock when they left in the morning from the roosting place. They were simply left behind. By the time the Swallows reached the end of the long Fly Away, almost half had been lost on the way.

But not Last One. He flew on to the end and found a well-earned place to live in some swamps near Johannesburg. He lived happily there, feeding on the insects that shared his reedy home. There were far more birds there than in England for migrants from all over Europe had made the great Fly Away and had settled in South Africa in the few places which suited them best. There was not so much food for each bird because what there was had to be shared amongst so many more. But it did not matter for the young birds were now fully grown and no longer needed growing-food. And the adult birds were not having families so they did not need extra food for their young.

Last One could not have really been very bright, for even in this pleasant place, he managed to get himself caught again by an ornithologist! He was out hunting amongst the reeds and did not see the net. But even if Last One was angry at being caught, the man who took him gently from the net was very pleased indeed.

'It's a ringed one!' he said excitedly, 'HS 89702 – from England.' Then he measured Last One, weighed him, then set him free. Soon there was a letter in the post from South Africa to England, announcing the arrival of a Very Important Bird – number HS 89702.

November, December, January and February passed very pleasantly in the swamp near Johannesburg. And then the birds became restless once again. This time the little bird voice seemed to be saying – 'Spring is coming. Fly home. Fly home!' And they all began to look longingly north, remembering the nesting places and the lush countryside which would soon be warm again after the winter cold. Once more all the migrant birds began to gather for the long flight. And then, one fine clear day, they were off on the Fly Home. This time northwards – always to the north.

Last One went with them of course, a big strong bird now and already on the lookout for a mate to share a nest and raise a family. The Fly Home was very like the Fly Away until the Swallows once more reached the Sahara Desert. On the way south they had been helped by a following wind. But now the wind was against them, which meant that they would need many thousands of wing beats more to reach the other side.

They had to fly all one day, then all night, then another day – and then another night! It was just after dawn when the Swallows reached the other end and waiting to greet Last One was – another ornithologist! This time, however, Last One did not fly into a net. He was so tired, that along with all the other completely exhausted birds, he flopped down into a tree which was growing beside a waterhole, and putting

his beak beneath his wing, he went straight off to sleep. There were rows and rows of sleeping birds, crowding every branch and twig of every bush and tree and the ornithologist was able to pick them up and examine them without them even waking up.

Last One was amongst them, of course, and soon another message was on its way to England, telling of the safe arrival back of HS 89702.

It was a fine summer day beside a stream near Norwich. The sun shone and there was the sound of insects buzzing all around. Gnats, flying beetles, river flies, even butterflies and silver-glinting dragonflies. It was a Swallow's paradise. Yet from a nearby barn there came the voice of a Swallow which was not enjoying life at all. It was a very angry Swallow which flew, time and again, out of the barn and into a nearby tree and then back again into the barn, calling all the time for its family to come out and see what a fine world it was outside.

The Swallow's mate flew round, not interfering. And inside the barn, in a beautifully made nest on a roof beam, four little Swallow fledglings were also quiet. They sat in the nest and it clearly did not matter to them that their father was so angry. The nest was comfortable, they were being very well fed and there seemed little reason why they should bother about the great world outside.

It could have been, of course, that they were just lazy. Or even that they were not very bright. Or it might just have been that the Swallow so angrily trying to get them out of the nest was Last One – it might have been just a case of 'like father, like son'. Who can tell?

Last One was a real Swallow. It was caught and ringed as a young bird on 23 August 1969 at Earlham, Norwich and ring no. HS 89702 was attached. It was caught again on November 2, the same year at Skinnerspruit by ringers working in a reed bed and it was found again on 30 June 1970, only four miles away from where it was first ringed at Earlham. It had flown more than 12,000 miles before its second birthday!

2 The Inside Story

HOW MANY BIRDS?

Birds are with us all the time. Even in the centre of cities there are Sparrows and Pigeons hopping or strolling about on the pavements. Town buildings are often used as comfortable roosting places for thousands of Starlings which come swarming in from the country every night. In the country, of course, we see them everywhere. But how many are there altogether?

This is what a lighthouse keeper on the island of Heligoland saw one night when birds were migrating:

'The whole sky is now filled with a babel of hundreds of thousands of voices and under the intense glare of the light, swarms of larks, starlings and thrushes career around in

ever-varying numbers like showers of brilliant sparks or huge snowflakes driven by a gale, continuously replaced as they disappear by freshly arriving multitudes.

'Such a migration stream lasts through a whole long autumn night and may be repeated for several nights in succession. Many birds dash headlong into the glass of the lantern and are stunned or killed. After a big migration night birds have been found lying five or six deep all round the lighthouse balcony.'

It has been worked out that at least 2,000 million birds leave Europe for Africa each autumn. This means that at least 500,000 birds cross every mile of the coast of North Africa for two whole months. Most birds fly at night but some like the Swallows use daylight for most of the way. All, however, as you read in the story, have to fly both by day and by night when they cross the Sahara Desert.

WHY THEY MIGRATE

Not all birds fly away to warmer lands in autumn. Many, like Sparrow on the cover, are stay-at-homes, or 'resident' birds. Others fly away only if the weather becomes so bad – ice and snow, for example, or floods – that they cannot find enough food. These are called 'partial migrants'. Birds that live entirely on insects find that all their food quickly disappears as winter comes, so they always have to fly away. It all depends upon whether birds can find enough to eat in winter whether they migrate or not. Here are lists of some birds in the three groups:

RESIDENTS

Little Grebe	Little Owl	Wren
Eider Duck	Tawny Owl	Dartford Warbler
Partridge	Kingfisher	Hawfinch
Pheasant	Green Woodpecker	Bullfinch
Herring Gull	Longtailed Tit	House Sparrow
Collared Dove	Nuthatch	Red Grouse
Barn Owl	Tree Creeper	

PARTIAL MIGRANTS

Heron	Snipe	Meadow Pipit
Mallard	Curlew	Song Thrush
Tufted Duck	Dunlin	Blackbird
Moorhen	Blackheaded Gull	Robin
Lapwing	Woodpigeon	Chaffinch
Ringed Plover	Skylark	Tree Sparrow
Golden Plover	Grey Wagtail	

MIGRANTS

Garganey	Cuckoo	Tree Pipit
Whimbrel	Nightjar	Sedge Warbler
Common Sandpiper	Swift	Reed Warbler
Lesser . Black-backed	Swallow	Whitethroat
Duck	House Martin	Nightingale
Common Tern	Sand Martin	Spotted Flycatcher
Turtle Dove	Yellow Wagtail	Willow Warbler

WHERE THEY GO

If you want to know where birds go when they migrate, there are three ways to find out. One is to follow them in an aeroplane. Another is to see them go off and then have somebody waiting at the other end to see them arrive. This is, of course, the method of 'ringing' which is what made the story of Last One possible. The third way is to track them by radar. Birds have been followed by light aeroplanes but they are very difficult to see and, of course, it is difficult to make an aeroplane fly slowly enough to keep them in sight. The third way of watching them, by radar, is much more successful, but of course, only short sections of birds flight can be followed – that is when they are within range of the radar scanners. The only really sure way of knowing where birds end up when they go off on their migrations is to fit rings to them and have watchers on the lookout for them at each end of their flights.

HOW RINGING WORKS

Birds have first to be caught for ringing and some very

cunning traps have been invented which catch birds without doing them any harm. One, called the Heligoland trap because it was first used on that island, lures birds into an open funnel of fine wire netting with a box at the end where the birds are caught. This is how it works. The birds see a fine feeding place beside a small pond where they can drink and perhaps have a bath. There are guide walls on each side of the feeding place leading to a funnel. The birds are gently driven into the funnel and when they are well inside, a swinging door is closed behind them. They now find a ramp in front of them which they land on and walk up into a box with a glass front which makes them think there is a way out ahead. When they are in the glass-fronted box, the ornithologist can easily lift them out through a door in the side.

Sir Peter Scott at the Wildfowl Trust at Slimbridge uses an even more cunning device. A big strong lightweight net is folded and arranged at one side of a place where birds feed. Electrically fired rockets are fixed to the net and when they are set off they carry it in a big sweeping arc over the feeding birds. The net falls on to the birds so that they can be caught without any injury.

When the birds are caught a careful note is taken of what kind of bird they are, how big, and whether male or female. Then a small metal ring is fixed to one leg. On the ring a little message is written – stamped into the metal. For example, it might say: 'Inform Brit. Museum, London, 3067972.' If the bird is found by somebody – it might be caught at a bird observatory somewhere else in the world, or found dead in the sea, or even by a roadside, knocked over by a passing car – the hope is that the person who found the bird will write to that address, saying where the bird was found. The number on the metal ring will have been written down in a book at the Museum giving the date when that bird's ring was put on. It will then be easy to see how far the bird has flown in the meantime and how long it took to get there. Very like a balloon race at a summer fête when toy balloons are set off with address tags tied to them to see how far they travel before bursting and coming to earth.

Heligoland trap

The chances of a ringed bird being found, of course, are very small and only a very few rings are returned in this way. From the start of ringing in 1909 until 1959, about two million birds were ringed in Britain but only about 50,000 were recovered. This means that of every two hundred birds caught and ringed, only five are ever seen again. But, of course, every one of those five birds tells a very important story. We know at once exactly how far the bird has flown since the ring was fixed to its leg. You read in the story how the Swallows fly all the way to South Africa – and back. Other migrant birds go to different places. For example: Blackbirds spending their summers in South Norway, fly to England for the winter.

Some birds nest and raise their families right up in the Arctic. They come to Britain in our winter because the Arctic is too cold even for them. There are many of these birds but the best known are the Snow Bunting, the Brent Goose and the Fulmar.

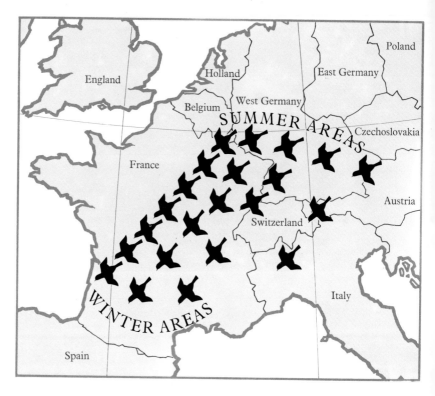

Migration of Blackbirds in winter

HOW BIRDS FIND THEIR WAY

When aeroplanes were first invented, their pilots had great difficulty in finding their way and often became lost. The pilots tried to solve their problems by having a magnetic compass like those used in ships. This gave them the direction of North. By simply flying in exactly the opposite direction they could fly south. By fitting a ring round the compass with all the other directions marked on it, they were able to fly in any direction they liked. But – that was not much use to a pilot unless he knew where he was when he started to fly and also the exact direction of the place he was going to, how far it was there and how long it would take to make the journey. He needed a map. But even this was not much use unless he could see the ground and compare the features he could see with those on the map.

Arctic Circle

Asia

Arctic Ocean

North
America

Greenland

Europe

Atlantic
Ocean

Africa

South
America

Probable routes of summer visitors from Africa

Probable routes of winter visitors from the Arctic regions

Probable routes of migrating seabirds flying to Britain to breed

Routes taken by birds visiting Britain

In other words, even though a pilot with a compass could fly his aeroplane in a straight line in any given direction, if there was fog or it was dark or for any reason he could not see the ground, he would quickly get lost.

Aeroplane pilots solved their problems in due course, using radio at first, then radar. Nowadays they know exactly where they are, their height, speed, and even if there are any other aeroplanes nearby, and, they can do all this without being able to see the ground at all.

Migrant birds have exactly the same problems to solve as pilots but they have no gadgets to help them at all. Not even a compass. So how do they find their way, flying by day or by night, over seas and deserts with no landmarks to help them? It is a problem that has puzzled ornithologists for years and they have now uncovered a lot of clues which are leading to a solution of the mystery.

WHAT DIRECTION TO FLY?

As you read in the story, all birds seem to get excited when the time comes for them to fly off. They chatter a lot together and flutter their wings. Some ornithologists noticed this and they wondered whether, perhaps, it had something to do with preparations for the long flight. So they carried out some tests.

Starlings just about to migrate south from England in October were caught and put into a cage. They all gathered at once in the southwestern corner of the cage and faced in the direction they would have been flying if they had not been caught! It did not matter if the cage was moved about or even if the sides were covered so that only the sky could be seen. They still stared anxiously in one direction – towards Africa!

In the following spring, the Starlings were still in their cages and they were watched again as the time came when they would normally be starting to fly to Britain for the summer. This time they began to head north east for about ten days and then they settled in a northwestern direction for the whole of the time it would have taken them to fly from Africa. It was thought that the Starlings must be finding their flying direction from the sky so, to test this, a sort of tub with windows round it was built. It was seen that when the light from the sun was allowed into the cage from all the windows, the Starlings headed northwest.

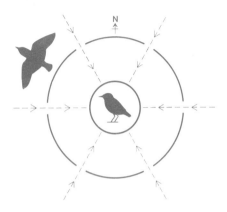

If, however, the light coming in through the windows was first reflected in mirrors (so that it seemed to be coming from a different direction) the Starlings changed their heading.

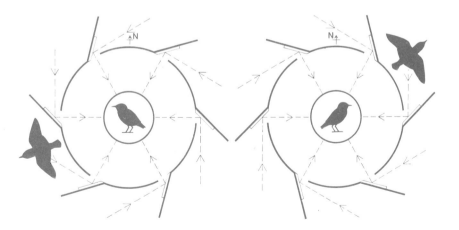

If all the windows through which the sun could shine directly were covered and a mirror used to direct it into one window only it was found that the Starlings would change their heading to what they now thought northwest to be.

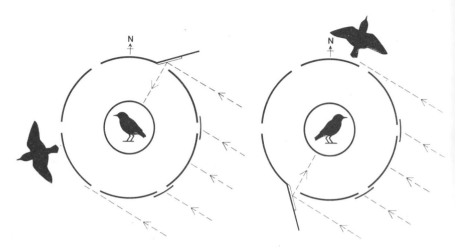

If the sun was hidden by thick cloud, however, the birds just did not head in any particular direction at all. They seemed to lose all sense of direction.

All these tests proved that the birds use the sun, in daylight, to find the direction in which they should fly when they migrate. But what about the birds that fly at night. How do they find the correct course to fly?

Some Mallard Ducks in America were taken three miles away from where they lived in the Illinois River Valley and released at night with tiny electric lights fitted to them so that their

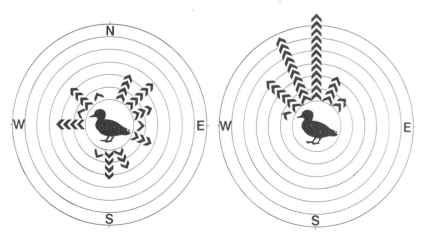

flight could be seen from the ground. On the first night, the sky was covered by cloud and the ducks all got lost! The test was made again, the ducks were released at the same place but this time there was a clear, starlit sky. This time they all flew straight home!

It was clear from this that the Mallards were using the star patterns in the sky to help them find their way. But just to make sure, some other birds were tested in a planetarium. If you have never seen a planetarium, imagine a big circular room with a domed ceiling. Little dots of light to represent stars are shone on to the dome from a very special kind of slide projector. It has several lenses and lights so that the whole night sky, as it is at any time of the year, can be shown on the dome, exactly like the real sky at night.

Blackcaps fly at night when they migrate and one of these was taken into the planetarium at the time it would normally be migrating to its nesting place and, sure enough, when it was released, it tried to fly north east. That, of course, was the planetarium north east. Other night-flying birds were tested in the same way and the star picture on the dome was changed so that it faced in a different direction. Once, the planetarium sky was shown so that the north star was in exactly the opposite direction to the real north star in the night sky outside. But the birds released in the planetarium still flew in the direction of north west as shown by the star pattern inside. If the planetarium sky was covered with 'cloud' the birds just flew about at random.

It is certain, therefore, that birds can find their way at night by the patterns of stars in the sky.

There is, however, a great mystery still to be solved. The sun and the stars appear to move in the sky at a set rate. This, of course, is really because the earth is revolving round its axis and things outside the earth only 'seem' to move. If you have a clock, you can say exactly where the sun should be at any time of the day (at midday, as everybody knows, it is at its highest point in the sky), and the same with the stars. But even if you have a clock, a very difficult sum has still to be done to work out, from the position of the sun, exactly where you are on the surface of the earth.

We have an internal clock. We wake up at about the same time each day, we feel sleepy at about the same time, and hungry too when meals are due! Birds have an internal clock which tells them when to wake up and sing and when to settle down for the night. The mystery, which nobody has yet been able to solve is – how do birds use their internal clock to find out from the sun and stars what direction to fly, across seas and deserts and at night? You really need to be a bird to answer that. A rather clever one.

BUMP OF LOCALITY

Birds have very sharp sight. Probably three times sharper than ours. Imagine being able to see three times better than you can now. You would be able to read this writing three times further away than you can now. Why not try it. Place the book where you can just read the words. Now move back three times that distance. Look around you. *Everything* you see would be three times clearer to a bird and the writing in this book could be easily read.

Are you good at remembering places you have seen before? Some people are and then they are said to have a good 'bump of locality'. Birds seem to have excellent bumps of locality which means that they quickly recognise places they have seen before.

Tests to prove this were done in Canada. Two Gannets (sea birds), were caught at Bonaventure Island in eastern Canada. They were taken to the places shown on this map and then released. They were followed by watchers in an aeroplane who drew the path they flew on a map. The map shows the tracks they drew.

You can see how they flew round in wide circles. You can imagine them looking round, with that wonderfully sharp sight, for some place they had seen before. Directly they found something they recognised, they were off at once, almost straight home.

These tests proved that birds, because of their good bump of locality and their good sight, find their nesting places at the

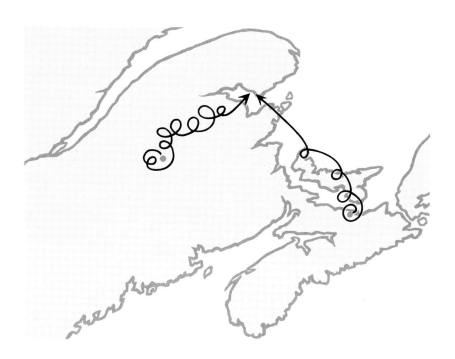

end of a long, long flight by recognising an area they have seen before.

WASTE OF LIFE
It is a pity to end the Inside Story with sadness. But nature is not always very kind. A great number of birds get lost and others simply fall into the sea or are eaten by birds of prey (hawks and eagles) on their long flights abroad. But this has to happen.

Suppose that all those millions of birds that cross the coast of Africa each year (two billion, remember?), succeeded in raising all their chicks. Supposing all those pretty eggs we see in nests became grown-up birds. Instead of two billion birds leaving Europe each year, there would be ten billion the first year and fifty billion the second! Within three years there would be so many birds in the world that we poor humans would starve to death for the birds would take all our fruit and corn and vegetables, just to stay alive!

But that does not happen. Some call it the 'balance of nature'. Others call it the hand of God. Whatever the cause, the fact is that thousands and thousands of young birds – and old ones too – die on their way to and from Africa. At the same time, thousands more die in Britain because in winter there is not enough food to go round. The result is that the total number of birds in the world stays more or less the same. And they all have a fair share of cherries in our orchards, raspberries in our gardens, corn in our fields.

But they are worth it, those long distance fliers. They make Britain a nicer place to live in with their songs and pretty plumage. But when you see the summer visitors in your garden remember that many of them have made that long flight to Africa and back again just to raise their brood. Be kind to them. They are really very brave little birds.

3 See Where it Happens

Britain is a very good place to see birds. This is because we are on their 'cross-roads'. In the spring and summer many birds arrive from their winter homes in Africa to make their nests in Britain. Swallows, Swifts, Cuckoos, Nightingales, Sand Martins, and many others do this and some, like Knots, Curlews, Sandpipers and Dunlins just call in on their way up to the Arctic to breed. All these birds fly north and south. Then in the autumn and winter Starlings, Blackbirds, Redwings, Chaffinches and different types of geese and duck begin to arrive just as the summer visitors are going back to Africa. Our winter guests come down from the Arctic and across from north Europe and Russia. They fly east and west. They migrate here to escape the cold winters in these places.

All these birds have to fly across the sea and over the coast to

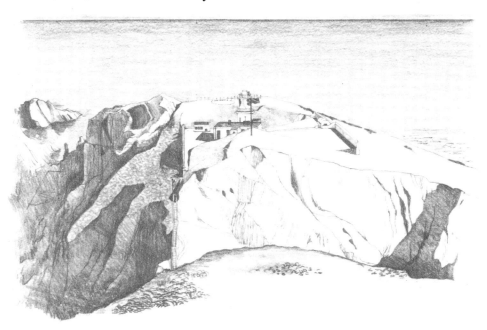

Lundy Island

Brownsea Island

arrive here. Some of the best places on the coast for seeing them have been made into proper bird sanctuaries and observatories. The National Trust owns several of these. Here is a list of National Trust reserves where you can see birds.

CAMBRIDGESHIRE
Wicken Fen
Although this nature reserve is not on the coast, it has many visiting birds every year. There are Heron, Shoveller, Goosander and many others.

DEVON
Arlington Court
In the grounds of the house there is a bird sanctuary where you can see several types of visiting wildfowl.
Lundy Island
The island has an observatory and is an important sanctuary. Many migrating birds breed or pass through here including Kittiwakes, Fulmars and Manx Shearwaters.

DORSET
Brownsea Island
The nature reserve on the island has a heronry. Several types

of migrating wildfowl visit the lake. You must go with a guided party to see it.

ISLE OF MAN
Calf of Man
This is an important bird sanctuary. It has an observatory. Visitors include Guillemots, Razorbills, Kittiwakes, and Puffins.

ISLE OF WIGHT
The Needles Headland
This is now a bird sanctuary. Large numbers of migrating birds pass by during the year.

KENT
Sandwich Bay
This nature reserve is a good place to see migrating birds. March is the best month for seeing the first ones arrive.

NORFOLK
Blakeney Point
Blakeney is on the north coast of Norfolk. It is one of the best places in the country for watching migrating birds. You can see Common Tern, Little Tern, Oyster-catcher, Ringed Plover, Redshank, Shelduck.
Salthouse Broad
Local people call this area Arnold's Marsh. It is near Blakeney Point and also has many visiting birds. In spring and autumn you can see large numbers of waders here.
Scolt Head Island
Sandwich Terns come here in March all the way from West Africa. They usually stay until September. Then they fly back to Africa for the winter. You can also see Redshanks, Green-shanks, Oyster-catchers, Gannets, Kittiwakes, and Arctic Skuas.

NORTHUMBERLAND
Newton Pool
A small nature reserve where you can see many different types of visiting waders and ducks.

Farne Islands

These islands form a very important sanctuary for migrating birds. Up to twenty different species of sea birds nest here every year. You can get there by fishing boat from the harbour at Seahouses.

Lindisfarne Castle

Only the castle is owned by the National Trust, but it is part of the Lindisfarne National Nature Reserve. In winter you can see Brent Geese, Eider Duck and many other species here.

WALES

GWYNEDD
Cemlyn (Anglesey)
In winter many migrating wildfowl visit this sanctuary.

WEST GLAMORGAN
Port Enynon Point
A good place to see migrating seabirds.

Calf of Man

Lindisfarne

Whitford Burrows

In November and December you can see large numbers of Oyster-catchers arriving for the winter here.

NORTHERN IRELAND

COUNTY DOWN

Blockhouse and Green Islands

Here you can see the Common Tern, Arctic Tern and Roseate Tern. The Arctic Tern spends the winter in the Antarctic. This is a journey of 10,000 miles!

Strangford Lough

The whole lough is now a nature reserve. It is possible to see tern, duck, geese, swan and waders here. Several places around the shore have been specially prepared as observation points.

The National Trust owns many places on the coast which are not nature reserves but which are excellent sites for watching birds migrating at different times of the year. Here is a list of them.

Ballymacormick Point, County Down
Seven Sisters, East Sussex

Fair Head and Murlough Bay, County Antrim
Kete, Dyfed
St Bride's Bay, Dyfed
St Catherine's Point, Isle of Wight
St David's Head, Dyfed
Lizard Point, Cornwall
Prawle Point, Cornwall
East Head, West Wittering, West Sussex

These are marked on the maps on pages 44–45 and 46–47. You will also find some other places marked which are not owned by the National Trust.

If you are interested in learning more about birds and their migration you can join the Young Ornithologists' Club. It is part of the Royal Society for the Protection of Birds, The Lodge, Sandy, Bedfordshire.

Cemlyn

Hilbre Island

October:
waders

Tatton Park

Bardsey
autumn:
*chats
warblers*

St. Davids
Head

Ramsey
Island

St. Brides
Bay

Skomer

Grassholm
gannets

Kete

Skokholm

Whitford
Burrows

Port Eynon
Point

Lavernock
Point

Slimbridge
Wildfowl
Trust

winter: *white-front
geese, duck, peregrin*

Brean
Down

Chew
Reservoir

Lundy
Island

Arlington
Court

Brown
Island

St. Ives
Head

Portland Bill

Porthgwarra

Lizard Point

Prawle Point

Slapton Ley

Start
Point

South Coast Headlands
spring: *seabirds and migrant*
autumn: *migrants*

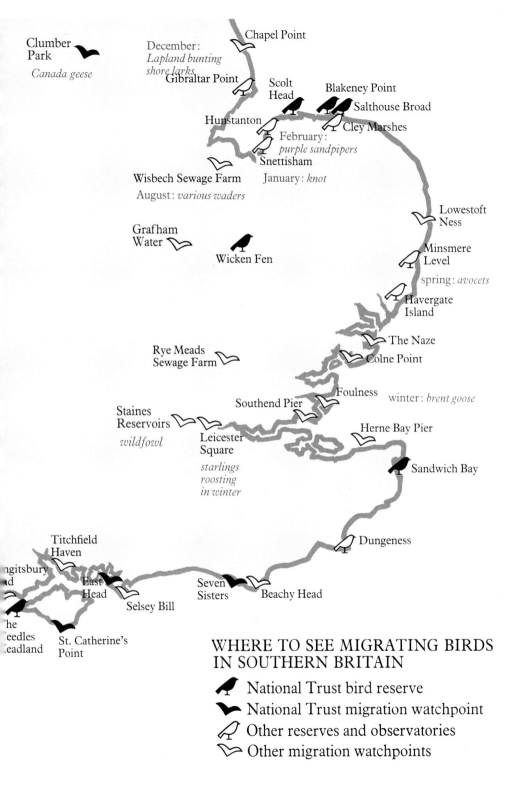

Clumber
Park
Canada geese

December:
*Lapland bunting
shore larks*
Gibraltar Point

Chapel Point

Scolt
Head

Blakeney Point
Salthouse Broad
Cley Marshes

Hunstanton

February:
purple sandpipers
Snettisham

Wisbech Sewage Farm   January: *knot*

August: *various waders*

Lowestoft
Ness

Grafham
Water

Wicken Fen

Minsmere
Level

spring: *avocets*

Havergate
Island

Rye Meads
Sewage Farm

The Naze
Colne Point

Foulness   winter: *brent goose*

Southend Pier

Staines
Reservoirs
wildfowl

Leicester
Square

*starlings
roosting
in winter*

Herne Bay Pier

Sandwich Bay

Titchfield
Haven

ngitsbury
d

East
Head

Selsey Bill

Seven
Sisters   Beachy Head

Dungeness

he
eedles
eadland

St. Catherine's
Point

WHERE TO SEE MIGRATING BIRDS
IN SOUTHERN BRITAIN

National Trust bird reserve
National Trust migration watchpoint
Other reserves and observatories
Other migration watchpoints

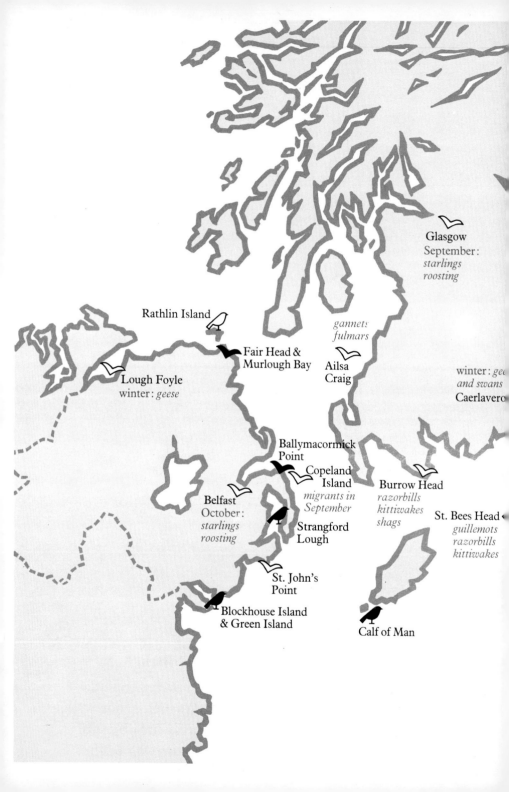

Glasgow
September:
*starlings
roosting*

Rathlin Island

*gannets
fulmars*

Fair Head &
Murlough Bay

Ailsa
Craig

Lough Foyle
winter: *geese*

winter: *gee
and swans*
Caerlavero

Ballymacormick
Point

Copeland
Island
*migrants in
September*

Burrow Head
*razorbills
kittiwakes
shags*

St. Bees Head
*guillemots
razorbills
kittiwakes*

Belfast
October:
*starlings
roosting*

Strangford
Lough

St. John's
Point

Blockhouse Island
& Green Island

Calf of Man

WHERE TO SEE MIGRATING BIRDS IN NORTHERN BRITAIN

National Trust bird reserve
National Trust migration watchpoint
Other reserves and observatories
Other migration watchpoints

Bass rock *eider duck*
gannets

Aberlady Bay
October:
dunlin
redshank

Lindisfarne Castle

Lindisfarne National
Nature Reserve
eider duck
brent geese
whooper swan
spring:
chiffchaffs
wheatears
swallows
whitethroats

Farne Islands

Newton Pool

Hauxley

Creswell Ponds

Seaton Sluice

Grune Point
September:
willow warblers

Heugh Battery

Hartlepool Bay January: *common scoter*
August: *skua*
Redcar
October: *purple sandpiper*
December: *roosting gulls*

Bempton Cliffs
July: *gannets*
Leighton Moss
razorbills
Flanborough Head
guillemots

Fairburn Ings
September:
¼ *million swallows and*
sand martins gather for
flight back to Africa

Humber Wildfowl
Refuge
winter: *pink-*
footed geese

Spurn Head
many common
migrants

Tetney Haven